KARMA
AND YOU

KARMA
AND YOU
CREATE YOUR OWN DESTINY

RAM K. SHARMA

RUPA

Published by
Rupa Publications India Pvt. Ltd 2022
7/16, Ansari Road, Daryaganj
New Delhi 110002

Sales centres:
Allahabad Bengaluru Chennai
Hyderabad Jaipur Kathmandu
Kolkata Mumbai

Copyright © Ram K. Sharma 2022

The views and opinions expressed in this book are the author's own and the
facts are as reported by him which have been verified to the extent possible,
and the publishers are not in any way liable for the same.

All rights reserved.
No part of this publication may be reproduced, transmitted,
or stored in a retrieval system, in any form or by any means,
electronic, mechanical, photocopying, recording or otherwise,
without the prior permission of the publisher.

P-ISBN: 978-93-5520-455-4
E-ISBN: 978-93-5520-457-8

10 9 8 7 6 5 4 3 2 1

Printed in India

This book is sold subject to the condition that it shall not,
by way of trade or otherwise, be lent, resold, hired out, or otherwise
circulated, without the publisher's prior consent, in any form of binding or
cover other than that in which it is published.

*Dedicated to my revered guru,
Shri Shri Paramahansa Yogananda
and
my parents,
the late Smt Bhuri Devi Joshi
and
the late Shri Ram Dyal Joshi*

Contents

Preface	ix
Prologue	xi
How I Discovered Karma	1
Definition of Karma	14
What Is Karma?	16
Karmic Account	20
Karma Chakra	24
Family Karma	29
Spousal Karma	34

Karma Towards Parents	37
Collective Karma	40
Corporate Karma	44
Karma for Wealth	50
Karma for Truth	57
Healing Karma	61
Karma and Thought	65
Karma and Your Personality	69
Karmas That Are Confusing	72
Karma of Goodness	75
Karma and Food	78
Karma and Arrogance	82
Karma and Gossip	86
Karma: Free Will and Destiny	90
Divine Karma	95
Towards Karmic Balance	98
Bibliography	101

Preface

One day, while sitting in meditation, a thought came to me: *I should write about karma*. But I am not a writer, per se; and so I cast the thought aside. As I was continually busy running our family business, I got no time to sit quietly or to write. The thought, however, persisted and it would crop up in my mind again and again.

Then came the dreadful COVID-19 pandemic. We all had to stay at home for a long time. I decided to make use of my time, and finally sat down to write the book on karma. It took me many months to complete.

KARMA AND YOU

While I was writing the book, I often knew exactly what I wanted to say. And whenever I sat down to meditate, I immersed myself in thought; and gradually I started to realize the many aspects of karma. Of course, all my life I have been a student of karma and have studied its ramifications.

Here, I have finally put my thoughts on paper.

Prologue

My father was a Karma Yogi. He was a very disciplined person. Throughout my childhood, I saw him take the correct decisions, even in difficult situations. He regularly invited learned persons to visit our family. Interactions with them helped us learn about many things.

This book contains many examples from his life, which was spent in acting towards the *right* karma. Some of these I have witnessed for myself, and some I have learned about from my elder brothers. In many ways this was a great learning for me. I was at an impressionable age and it had a positive impact on me. At that time, I did not have a full understanding about karma but got a little introduction—all without knowing the full ramifications.

Here is one such example:

It was 1942. The freedom movement was in full swing. The Congress had called for a Quit India movement against the British government. They planned to launch the movement from Calcutta. Sensing trouble, the British imposed Section 144 in the city; and none of the movement leaders were allowed to enter the city. There were announcements that if they tried to enter the city, they would be stopped and arrested at the border. Anybody harbouring them would be fined and arrested as well.

However, the leaders decided to go ahead with the movement anyway. They came into the city, disguised as truck drivers and coolies. My father opened the gates to the Baidyanath Head Office at 1, Gupta Lane, Kolkata, to shelter and house

PROLOGUE

the movement leaders. Several prominent leaders such as Binodanand Jha, Kedar Pandey and others took shelter there.

My father took a personal and a business risk when he opened the gates and sheltered the leaders of the movement. But he thought that it was the right thing to do and a karmic act towards his country.

All these leaders ultimately managed to assemble together to start the Quit India movement. They were later arrested and put behind bars. Most of the leaders who stayed at the Corporate House before Independence went on to lead the country after it attained freedom, as chief ministers and cabinet ministers. These leaders always had great respect for the company.

I was lucky to be born into such a family.

How I Discovered Karma

MY FIRST INTRODUCTION TO KARMA

Three personal experiences changed my perception on life and introduced me to the concept of karma. I keenly witnessed and learned about how the concept works.

In the first instance, I was a young boy, around the age of twelve, when my mother took me to meet a sadhu—a yogi, popularly known as Devraha Baba. Some people used to say that he was over a hundred and twenty years old. He had a vast following. The first President of India, Dr Rajendra

Prasad, used to visit him as well.

When I met Baba ji, he called me by my first name and said, 'Ram Krishan, so you have come.'

I was quite astounded. I did not remember meeting him before or telling him my name. My mother then told me that she had brought me to meet him before, when I was younger. I also witnessed him calling almost everybody who came to see him by their first names. He seemed to have an exemplary memory, even at this advanced age.

He was sitting on a small shack, elevated by twelve feet and made of bamboo, leaves and wood. He wore only a deerskin around his waist, even in the cold winter of Allahabad. I noticed that he talked to everyone in a similar fashion, whether they were rich or poor. This fascinated me. I had never before seen a sadhu—or even a normal person treating all who came to meet him in the same manner.

But Baba ji treated them all alike. He did not accept any donations. He did not touch money. However, if people brought him some fruits, he would keep one of the items and distribute the rest to the people around him. He had a very simple and frugal lifestyle.

While talking to my mother, Baba asked her a question about my uncle, Shri R.N. Sharma, a man who had built a complimentary guest house (dharamshala) in Vrindavan for the visiting pilgrims. He laughingly asked her whether the pilgrims complained when they stayed at the rest house and ate the food available there.

My mother and I were taken aback. Reluctantly, she said, 'Yes, sometimes they complain that there should have been more of this or that—even though everything is complimentary.'

He then started to laugh.

He said that we should remember that this is the paradox of life. 'The pilgrims behaved in this manner because it is their negative karma that is complaining, even though you are serving them unselfishly. However, you should not be deterred from doing your karma. You must continue to give the pilgrims shelter and feed them. This is *your* karma. You should not be discouraged even if they are complaining. Complaining is *their* karma.'

This struck me as very odd. After all, how can people grumble when they receive free food and shelter? And why should we not care about it and continue to do the work we've set out to do?

Devraha Baba

HOW I DISCOVERED KARMA

This got me thinking about karma and what it means. The concept, since then, has always remained embedded in my mind.

MY LESSON ABOUT KARMA

A while ago, I was at Dehradun in order to attend my daughter's annual school function at Welham Girls' School. We were staying at my sister-in-law's house. In the afternoon I had nothing to do; as recommended by Rashmi, my wife, I picked up a book—*An Autobiography of a Yogi* by Shri Shri Paramahansa Yogananda.

I read through the book, in turns fascinated and deeply moved. He, much like Baba ji, wrote about karma, its positive and negative sides and how it could affect our lives. It made a lasting impact on me and completely changed how I perceived life thereafter. I then read all the books he had written and understood how karma works in our lives. From that day onwards, I mentally acknowledged

Shri Shri Paramahansa Yogananda as my guru. After this, I started to meditate with his blessings.

Henceforth, I started observing my family and myself through the lens of karma and the results were amazing! I closely watched and noticed the actions of my immediate family, my relatives, friends and colleagues, paying attention to what they did, how they behaved and what was the corresponding effect on their lives. The implications were uncanny!

I saw that the results of their actions were accurately related to their karmic actions. I sometimes could even predict what would happen after observing a particular karmic action. Soon, noticing and observing people around me became a passion.

In this book, I have provided many real-life examples of what I have observed about karma and its ramifications during my lifetime. Karma has also made me reconsider many decisions in

HOW I DISCOVERED KARMA

my own life. I have always tried to do right and often, I have had to stop, think and change the course of my actions to correct them and bring myself on to the right path.

Then, after many years, I personally experienced an amazing incident as a result of my own karma!

Shri Shri Paramahansa Yogananda

THE PROOF

When I was in my fifties, I got the chance to experience an amazing miracle—a karmic miracle!

I was running a family business in Kolkata. At the time, the state was under communist rule. Labour laws were biased towards the workers and taking any kind of disciplinary action without prior government approval was impossible.

I, too, had inherited an undisciplined and arrogant labour union. The members would not allow any positive changes in the unit, nor would they increase production. They would agitate, shout and often go on strike.

They held us, the employers, to ransom.

Our senior managers wanted to start many cases against them and deeply desired to control them. I had personally decided that I would not take any wrong and unethical steps against the members of the union despite the situation.

We suffered. Growth stopped. I had to build another factory to meet the increasing demand. We tried to cooperate with the union and were good to them. When the workers had personal or health-related problems, we helped them, but all this benevolence had no effect on their behaviour. I could see where this was going: the workers were on the wrong path, and their mass negative karmic actions would have an effect.

One day, the union went on a strike in response to a disciplinary action taken by Mr Ghosh, the unit head. We consulted our legal advisor who advised that we should declare a lock out at the factory to discipline the workers. However, I decided against a factory lockout. We kept our factory and head office open. A few senior staff members showed up for work, but the workers continued to sit outside and shout slogans.

We supplied the market, making use of the other new unit in the state and units outside our state. At the end of the month, all the senior employees at the factory and at the head office received their salary. Since the workers had not showed up for work, they did not get any salary. The same thing happened the next month. When two months passed in the same manner, the workers started to fight among themselves.

Some of the workers started to say that since the factory was open, they should go in and work. The primary argument being that they needed their salaries. However, there was another section of workers who stopped their peers from entering the factory. This fuelled further disagreement, with several workers saying that since the management had decided against a factory lockout and were indeed asking everybody to work and earn their salaries, they would prefer to get back to work.

'They have not done anything to harm us, then why should we stop working and support the protest for action taken against a single worker?'

A fight ensued within the union. It became very bad. Both the factions were very agitated and frustrated. Not knowing what to do, the union leaders decided to teach the management a lesson. They decided to send us a mass resignation letter, hoping that the company would be unable to run the unit without them and that we would have to reverse our disciplinary action. In a burst of anger, they had drafted a resignation letter without even consulting their union lawyer and had handed it to our unit head.

We immediately rushed with this letter to our legal advisor. He told us that by the law of the country, if somebody makes an offer and it is accepted in writing, then it is a completely valid contract and cannot be rescinded. This is the law of contracts.

It was 2 p.m. in the afternoon. We immediately drafted the acceptance letter to the resignations for each and every employee. Our advisor told us that we should go to the General Post Office and post each letter and get a receipt and the postmaster's stamp on it. So, the company posted letters of acceptance to each and every employee and got the receipts.

The next morning, the workers realized what had happened. They immediately wanted to take back their resignation letters, but we told them that we had already accepted their resignation in writing, and had the receipts. When they rushed to their lawyer, he told them that nothing could be done now. We then paid full gratuity and dues and sent them away.

I saw all my labour problems disappear in a single day. It was like a miracle!

The law of karma had made this happen. The management had kept on the right path and the result was unbelievable. The workers and the union were on a negative path, hence karma made them take such a wild and arrogant decision.

After this situation passed, we had the best workers in our unit and managed to clock five times more production with the same manpower. We could not have imagined this in our wildest dreams. We were free of the unions troubling us without cause. The positive karma done by the company and the negative mass karma done by the union had this karmic effect on both the parties.

This incident gave me the proof I needed. I now knew what positive and negative karma could do. I was now a firm believer in the law of karma. I decided that I would try to follow the right path, to the best of my ability, for the rest of my life.

'Karma is the powerful law of cosmic cause and effect. Your past actions will determine what happens to you today.'

—*The Rig Veda*
Translated by Ralph T.H. Griffith

Definition of Karma

Karma comes from the Sanskrit word 'kri', which means 'to do'. Karma means 'action' and it is related to both our past lives and the present one. It begins with the understanding that every action has a consequence, whether in this life or in the future. At any time of their life, a person's present situation is the sum total of all his past karmic actions. Karma includes intentions, attitudes, actions and desires. Whenever any action is taken, a person must take responsibility. Whatever happens in this life is the response to the action he took in the past.

DEFINITION OF KARMA

The ultimate goal is to break the cycle of birth and death by doing the right karma. Thereby, a person may be absorbed into the divine.

One of the important concepts is that God has given us free will to undertake whatever karmic action we want. So the soul keeps learning with every action and reaction, every karma and its result. Karma is the supreme teacher.

'A man evolves through every constructive action he performs.'

—*Shri Shri Paramahansa Yogananda*

What Is Karma?

The world is governed by physical laws formulated by scientists like laws of gravity, relativity, motion and others. Scientists like Isaac Newton, Albert Einstein and others have proven these laws through observations and experiments. However, a different world also exists, one beyond physical laws. The ancient rishis of India experienced them and wrote about their experiences.

The law of karma is part of our spiritual world. This law has been explained in almost all kinds of spiritual writings, such as the Vedas, Upanishads,

WHAT IS KARMA

Gita, and in Buddhist teachings. One of the most important ancient books of India, the Bhagavad Gita contains lessons on the meaning and effects of karma in an extensive manner.

The rishis of ancient India observed, experimented and discovered the existence of karma. They found that the law of karma was as real and as strong as the physical laws of our universe.

The law of karma outlines that every action—mental, verbal or physical—has a consequence. None of us, no matter how rich, powerful or influential, can avoid these consequences. Each and every action or thought will have equal and appropriate ramifications.

Every human being, through thought and action, becomes the maker of his own destiny. Whatever energy/karma he sets in motion will return to him, forming a complete cycle, just like a boomerang. This occurs without fail.

Karma acts as a spiritual law of justice. It follows a man from incarnation to incarnation until the karmic account is balanced. The 'karmic account' can be understood as a massive memory bank which records all our actions—good and bad—from all our past lives. Our destiny depends on the positive or negative deeds collected from our past to our present lives.

The law of cause and effect operates with or without our approval. We are free to choose between the two alternatives—good and evil, right and wrong—at every step of our life.

WHAT IS KARMA

'Life is an echo. What you send out, comes back. What you sow, you reap. What you give, you get. What you see in others, exists in you.
Life always gets back to you.'

—*Zig Ziglar*

'Whatsoever a man soweth, that shall they also reap.'

—*The Holy Bible*

'Like gravity, karma is so basic, we often don't even notice it.'

—*Sakyong Mipham*

Karmic Account

An account of a person's every positive or negative action, utterance or thought is meticulously maintained by the spiritual universe.

Every karmic act in this lifetime (or in one's past lives) is recorded and the consequences then play out. Good karma produces joy and brings so-called 'luck' during a person's lifetime. Negative karma leads to sorrow, and the person will have to learn from the situation to balance his karmic account.

How are things added to our karmic account?

All actions, thoughts, choices and desires accumulate in this account. This account continues

KARMIC ACCOUNT

throughout our lifetimes until the karma is brought into a balance. Its fruition will always come at the right time for a person to learn and evolve.

If we accumulate a fat, positive karmic account, it will bring us peace, prosperity, good luck and happiness. If we create a bad karmic debt, it will bring us unhappiness in all forms.

Why does bad karma torment us?

It does so because of the spiritual universe, which can act as a guide and help us learn, get back on track, and lead a good life.

If we have very large debts in the form of negative karma, it may take many incarnations to clear it. Bad karma is always carried to the next life.

Here is a simple example: if we accumulate a lot of money and keep depositing it in our bank account, we can use it during times of financial crisis. In the same way, a good karmic account protects us, and helps us prosper and move past our obstacles.

However, if the account has a negative balance, then life will keep throwing challenges and obstacles for us to learn and correct our course. In such a case, we do not have the protection that a good karmic account may have provided.

Why is it that sometimes a negative action takes too long to give us a negative result?

It is because we have a lot of goodness in our karmic account; until it wears out, we are saved from its harsher effects. Once we have depleted our good karma, negative karma will then have immediate repercussions. People with no positive or negative karma in their accounts experience immediate consequences of their actions, whether positive or negative.

When a person has balanced the slate of positive and negative karma, his karmic slate becomes clean. Any positive or negative actions, henceforth, have immediate results.

KARMIC ACCOUNT

'Good and bad action in your past lives in turn forms the settings of (the) next incarnation.'

—*Shri Shri Paramahansa Yogananda*

Karma Chakra

When a man, wisely or unwisely, sets his karmic energies into motion, the consequences come full circle.

When a person does a good karmic act, he continuously reaps its positive benefits. Likewise, when he does a bad karmic act, negative results find their way to him.

How to avoid the trap of a bad karmic act? Let me give you an example. When a person who has been walking on the right path comes across someone who harms him, there is a tendency to retaliate and harm the perpetrator as well.

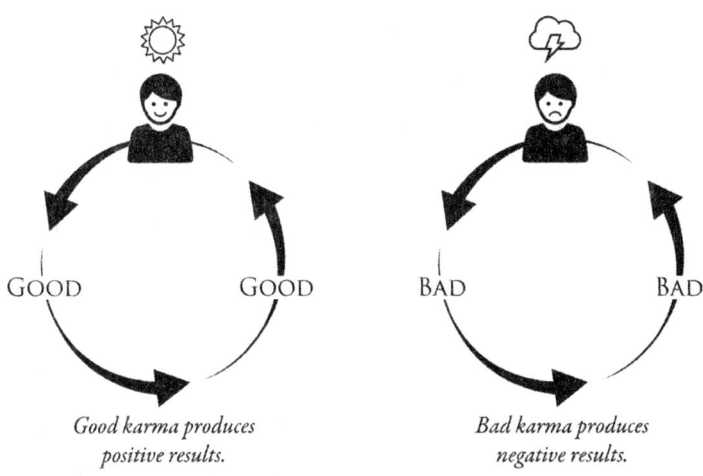

Good karma produces positive results.

Bad karma produces negative results.

Accordingly, if he acts to cause harm and seek revenge, he will leave his circle of good chakra and enter a cycle of bad chakra himself. He will, thus, create a new negative chakra for himself and will have to face its consequences thereafter. If, however, he does not respond negatively and avoids retaliation, he will continue to walk on the right path.

Such a person should not be agitated. He should remember that the person who has harmed him has entered a negative chakra and will reap the consequences. Such a person will definitely be the recipient of his own negative actions and his karma will give him the appropriate negative reaction. Simply put, the law of karma will take care of it.

Hence, if the harmed person does not enter a negative chakra, he will be unscathed by this incident. This explains why a person must always remain within his positive chakra and not be tempted to step out of it to take revenge. The lesson here is that one must refrain from negative actions, even if harm is being done.

Step aside. Let his negative karma take care of it. A person should not stray from his path and engage in wrongful actions. This is the best way to remain unaffected by negative karma, but a person should always follow his own path.

Let me give you a personal example of a family I once knew. The father was a hard-working and sincere man. He was always helping people around him. He was charitable and had a good standing in society. He was, simply, on the right side of karma.

One day, he fell ill. His son did not take care of him, did not consult the right doctors and did not take the illness seriously. After some time, the father died.

Now, many years later, the son who did not take care of his father too fell seriously sick. In this manner, karma worked its magic. He reaped what he sowed. The ill man's son too did not look after him. He suffered and died unhappy.

Such examples can be seen all around us. There is nothing in this world that is not subject to this law. We are all experiencing the present as a consequence of our past actions.

KARMA AND YOU

'What goes around comes around.'

—*Anonymous*

'How people treat you is their karma; how you react is yours.'

—*Wayne Dyer*

'You have to be careful when involving yourself with someone else's karma.'

—*Brownell Landrum*

Family Karma

Everyone wants a happy family. We want our children to be successful and blessed. But all of us are not equally fortunate to have such joy, and we must work towards it.

To start with, the husband and wife must be true to each other and act sincerely towards each other. This lays the foundation of the family. When one partner begins to cheat and fight, the bond begins to break down. This will lead to many unfortunate consequences, like unhappiness, ill health and worse. It may stop the two from enjoying physical and mental peace.

Once children are born into the family, they too get a dose of dishonest karma and learn from their parents. Children follow what they see and experience, and such an experience can ruin their lives as well. Some children, however, are mentally stronger. They do not get influenced by negativity around them and manage to carve out a positive path for themselves. Only a strong-willed child can overcome a negative environment.

These days, in a bid to keep the young ones happy and pacified, parents often end up giving their children all the luxury they demand. This is not good karma. All children must be disciplined. They must experience their own hardships to develop character and sow the seeds of good karma. The harder they are made to work—alongside love, affection and support—the more successful they will be. The law of karma never fails, and this should be explained to the growing minds.

The cumulative actions of a family constitute

the joint karma of the group. This karma has far-ranging effects according to the degree of their thoughts and actions—good and evil.

That you are born into a certain family is no coincidence. A soul takes birth in a certain family to fulfil the karmic debts of his past life, and he must do this with other souls born into the family. Whether the family is rich, creative, happy, powerful, spiritual or otherwise depends on what the soul of the child has come to learn; he has to balance his past karma.

When a child is born, it is the parents' duty to inculcate goodness and right thoughts from day one. This kind of atmosphere within the home will create karma for him and his siblings. The net karma, which is the sum total of the karmic actions of the entire family, will determine the family karma.

The net good karma of a family will result in happiness, prosperity, good health and growth for all the members of the family. They will learn from each other, grow in stature within society and will receive love and respect from all. On the other hand, a net negative cumulative family karma will result in unhappiness, disease and bad luck for all. The long-term happiness and prosperity of a family also depends on how the family conducts themselves with each other and in society.

It is very important for parents to realize this and teach their children good habits from the beginning. They should be taught to read inspirational books and stories, learn to treat all—whether rich or poor—with respect; they must know how to be grateful and modest. They must be encouraged to choose their friends wisely and be careful of the company they keep. Negative company can destroy all virtues.

Many times, a good soul is born into a family with previously accumulated bad karma. This is because the new soul must learn to stay calm and untouched, even in a bad environment. He has also come to help, improve and change the family karma of all the members.

In this manner, a family is always affected by negative or positive influences and thus creates its own destiny.

'God is not your judge. You are your own judge. Your destiny is in your hands and (so is) your karma.'

—*Anonymous*

Spousal Karma

It is said that marriages are made in heaven; they probably are. Each soul takes birth to learn something that it lacks. Life partners are chosen by the souls to help the other learn and complete their soul's journey, even as they themselves try to meet their own goals and complete themselves.

Matrimonial karma is a karmic relationship. In a marriage, one must understand each other's karmic needs. These needs, most of the time, are things that the other may be struggling with and something that is necessary for them to learn from the other.

SPOUSAL KARMA

Karmic learning can be done together, especially if both partners are lacking something. The couple can face problems together. There may be challenges in bringing up the children or other issues, but they must put their heads together and make joint efforts to solve them and learn from them.

Couples may face many problems, such as ill health, financial difficulties, jealousy and ego, issues of control and so on. As they go through life, the problems will change according to what they have learned and things that they are yet to learn.

In the form of a simple equation, consider that couple power is $1+1=2$. But when the partners act together and with positive karma, their life looks something like this: $1+1=11$.

This excess is the power of good karma. When they act together in unison, they become a force to reckon with!

Couples leading ethical and honest lives will convey the value of these virtues to their children. And these children will grow up to be hard-working and successful, and ultimately, they will bring happiness to the family in abundance.

Couples have to learn together. They must balance their karmic account by working with each other; or else they will return to the earth and be doomed to face the consequences again and again. They have to practise patience, honesty, love, understanding, sharing, etc. When two souls are sincerely connected in this manner, a fulfilling relationship is guaranteed!

'Every conscious activity you
perform will rule the
destiny of your life.'

—Shri Shri Paramahansa Yogananda

Karma Towards Parents

Almost all the faiths in the world believe in the existence of a divine father and a divine mother. We believe that they are impartial to all. Those who pray to these entities receive their mercy. It doesn't matter whether the one praying is good, bad or evil. All are God's children and God does not differentiate among earthlings.

And it is God who has imbued the law of karma with power.

God expects all children to be responsible towards their parents, to treat them with the same consideration that they were shown when they were young. He created parents on earth in his image. The earthly father and mother are here to act as representatives of our divine father and divine mother. Just as the divine father looks after the whole world as his children, the human father looks after his own earthly children. Among humans, the father is responsible for teaching his children the law of karma and instilling in them, with wisdom and love, all the good thoughts and the universal significance of good karmic actions.

Each parent loves their child, whether he/she is beautiful or ugly, fat or thin, intelligent or dull, good or bad. Even the evil are loved by their parents, who keep hoping and trying to change them for the better.

Hence, loving our parents and doing good karmic acts towards them is in fact a step closer to loving our divine father. Parents have been put on the earth by the divine father so we may learn to love him and reach salvation. If we cannot respect and love our parents, we will never learn to love our divine father. This is the first step humans must take to know God. Just like God loves each and every one unconditionally—good or bad—earthly parents also love their children.

In your life, you will notice that people who have performed good karmic acts towards their parents have generally received more success and joy. They have, in truth, come closer to our divine father and divine mother. If you want to find God, start with your parents—this is the right karma.

'Do not be scared of God;
be scared of your bad karma.'

—Swami Sivananda

Collective Karma

Joint or cumulative actions of people living in societies, countries or the planet add up to create our collective karma. The net good or bad karma done by such a large group has a strong effect on the communities that they live in. They have to face the collective consequences of their actions. These reactions can be felt at the local, regional, national and global levels.

The country creates good karma if its politicians and people are honest, make fair laws, impart good education, look after the poor, befriend their neighbours, be in tune with nature and use their

COLLECTIVE KARMA

resources for the well-being of all citizens. Such nations see growth, prosperity, good health and happiness all around. Such countries are never at war and believe in peace and harmony.

On the other hand, countries where the state and people are corrupt—who do not spend money on education, health, civil amenities, environmental welfare and do not treat *all* in a fair manner—society suffers there. In these nations, there often is a breakdown in law and order, and its cities are overtaken by hooligans. Ultimately, there will be no happiness, growth or prosperity in these nations.

The bad karmic conditions created by such collectives can even determine and influence the climate, the environment, which may lead to typhoons, storms, fires and earthquakes. All hatred, anger and evil vibrations can disturb the magnetic force of the earth and cause destruction and diseases.

The cumulative energy/karma of all nations together is known as global karma. God has given man the power of creation and destruction; we can either make something beautiful or trigger destruction. Everything that has happened to this day is recorded in the ether. Evil vibrations can upset the balance of the earth and the accumulated negative karma of the globe can even cause starvation, floods, tsunamis, earthquakes and epidemics. One of the examples in recent times is the outbreak of COVID-19.

The sum total of good karma will bring peace and harmony among nations. Hence, there will be no animosity or war among them.

So far, it appears that positive karma on earth is greater than the combined negative karma—that's why we are all alive today. We are all one universal family. Nationalism should be replaced by global patriotism. This karma will ensure that we all live in peace and enjoy happiness in the future.

COLLECTIVE KARMA

'If we send out positive loving energy, we will receive positive energy in return.'

—*Anonymous*

Corporate Karma

Business schools teach you how to run your company successfully. However, they do not teach you how to run it ethically. If a company operates with fairness and spirituality, then corporate karma becomes the work culture. This leads to long-term success. It is important to inculcate this equitable work culture in the management of the company.

Corporates must recruit people with good character, rather than with intelligence only. Employees with good character will create value and remain loyal to the organization in the long run. Their good karma will also add to the company's success.

Too often, smart corporate leaders only think of the short-term goals and larger profits for the company—even going as far as resorting to unethical means. In the long term, such an organization may suffer, even if it has good products, vast distribution channels and a smart workforce. This is because every action the management takes will impart good or bad karmic effects to the business.

The most successful people in a corporation are those who are humble, calm and honest. If they keep themselves focused on such good karmic acts, the organization will ultimately grow.

Once money becomes paramount, companies usually start becoming arrogant and self-centred. This is their downfall. Nobody likes arrogance; and people tend to notice the bad vibrations. Since karma always keeps the balances, a time will come when they will have to face their eventual decline.

This may cause loss of wealth, image and reputation.

You will feel the urge to do the wrong karmic acts for short-term gains in your ventures, but this will have a long-lasting, negative effect on the business. Instead, if you keep your mind stable and not let a bad situation or a weak moment push you to make a wrong decision, then you will witness miracles.

As a team, the company must impart the 'right thinking' into the company culture. A company with a good culture will attract good people and good karma will attract good employees to the organization.

The increasing role of competition and motivation for higher profits can sometimes eat into the foundation of the organization. All rules are then broken to deliver success and rise up in the stock market. Ultimately, companies that have succumbed to easy profits will crumble easily when a crisis hits them. On the other hand, companies with good karmic culture will survive.

CORPORATE KARMA

If you look at all the top companies of the world, such as Microsoft, Walmart, Alphabet, Rolex, Google, Sony, Tata, Infosys, Wipro, etc., you will see that all of them have great corporate social responsibility programmes and policies. The wealthiest businessmen of the world are also the most philanthropic. These businessmen have created good karmic companies that will continue to grow in the future.

My late father, Shri R.D. Joshi, was the co-founder of Baidyanath, an ayurvedic medicine manufacturing company, which has been running successfully for over a hundred years. Along with his younger brother, he started the company from scratch. Over the years, it grew to become one of the largest companies in its field. They must have done something right.

I believe that they worked with good karma. For example, my father had the right attitude towards helping other people. He used to tell us, his children: *'Your business is not only to earn money, but to cure people. Money will come automatically.'*

He used to run the business according to this philosophy and karmic thought. This yielded great results, and the business kept growing.

When a company pays all its suppliers in a fair and timely manner, it manages to get good quality products at lower rates than usual. This automatically yields higher profits and ensures that the company has a reliable network of loyal vendors. In times of crisis, the company is always supported by these loyal suppliers.

These values were part of our company's culture. Our company had a very efficient and ethical general manager, Shri Beni Prasad Sharma. Since childhood I saw him making payments to vendors punctually, every single time. The vendors were very happy. They became very loyal to the company.

I asked him why he took making timely payments so seriously. He told me that there were many benefits to doing so.

'Firstly, it is good karma to pay on time and not hold anybody's dues beyond the accepted time frame. This timely payment helps the company purchase at lower prices, which can be around 5 per cent to 7 per cent below the usual rates. If there is any shortage of raw materials, the dealers always consider our company's requirements on priority and ensure that there is no shortage. Because of timely payments, the company also always receives the best quality materials.'

The net result was that the company would get the right goods at the best prices, resulting in better margins than our competitors'.

Hence, here too, good karma makes for good business sense.

'Being good is good business.'

—Anita Roddick, co-founder of Body Shop

Karma for Wealth

A person is born into a rich or a poor family based on his actions and the karma of his past lives. Hence, he is personally responsible for his present well-being.

Wealth is not evil. It is how you use it that is important. This will determine your future material success. If wealth is used for good causes, you will get good results. When you use wealth for bad causes, it will bring you sorrow. Wealth that is used to aid others and support other good causes will ultimately grow.

Most business houses in India carve out a

percentage of their profits for charity. Some give 5 per cent, some 10 per cent and some even more. In the long run, companies that give more do better than the others.

I remember my father setting aside 10 per cent of his income for social causes. With this fund, he built a school in our village in Rajasthan. This school was free for the students. Students came from other surrounding districts too. Year after year, the school expanded. Soon, a playing field was added, then a hostel, and then teachers' living quarters were also added. This brought prosperity to the entire area. The school received the Best Rural School Award in the state for many years in a row.

In this manner, sharing your wealth with society should be a prime karmic consideration for corporations and business houses. It ultimately yields good results.

Karma that attracts money includes charity, generosity, gratitude, prompt payment of debts, sharing of wealth and more. With wealth comes duty—you must care for all the people around you. Your heart, and not your greed, should be the guide as you earn and spend money. Attachment to wealth does not bring more wealth. Only a large heart and good intentions bring positive results.

Many people spend a lot of money praying in order to attain more wealth, but only good karma can make you successful.

On the other hand, negative karma can ruin you. If you earn money by cheating, some day someone will cheat you. You will lose more than what you had gained in the first place. You must pay all your debts, because some day, karma will ensure you pay it with interest. Praying to God for more wealth even as you continue to make unethical decisions will not yield any benefits.

Money that has been wrongly gained has far-reaching consequences on your family and you, especially on your children. They may become spoiled and make a mess of their lives. Children follow the path taken by their parents, and this karma of self-indulgence will lead to the misery of the entire family.

Wealth that has been wrongly earned sometimes leads to expenditure. You may fall ill and have to unnecessarily spend on illness. You may have to fight more and more court cases. Your life will not be peaceful and happy.

I have seen many people with meagre pay lead honest lives. They have always been happy and healthy. Their children have also followed in their parents' footsteps and ultimately, they too have led a happy life. They go on to earn lots of money, make a good reputation and add to their good karma.

I would like to share a real-life experience to illustrate my point. We had an employee in our organization called Hari Prasad Sharma. Part of the company's middle-level management, he was an honest and hard-working man.

On noting his sincerity, I sent him to Delhi to supervise the construction of a house I was building there. He was put in charge of the construction and was to see that all the purchases were in order and bought at the best prices. When we checked the costs, we realized that he had managed to purchase all the materials at a rate that was lower than our budget and were still of good quality. We learnt that he personally went to the source and bought directly from them. We saved a lot of money because of his honesty and hard work. After a few years, he retired.

Much later, when we were planning another construction project, we immediately thought of him. I contacted him to see if he could come on in an advisory capacity to oversee the work. He said that both his sons did not want him to work any more. As I inquired into it, he said that his sons had done well—they had made their way up to top-level management in their respective organizations—and were earning millions. They also doted on him, their father, and insisted that there was no need for him to slog it out at work.

They wanted him to stay with them. He politely explained why he could not join the project and was rather apologetic about it—which further endeared him to me.

I realized that this was a karmic effect and the result of his honesty. His children must have imbibed his morality and sincerity. It had helped them reach high positions in their companies. Honesty pays!

'As soon (as) man begins to worship possessions, name and fame—he finds unhappiness. The best prayer to get more wealth is to use it in the right manner—money automatically flows in.'

—*Shri Shri Paramahansa Yogananda*

'Only income earned justly with hard work gives happiness to man.'

—*The Rig Veda*
Translated by Ralph T.H. Griffith

'Money earned through moral means, when used for good deeds, leads to salvation.'

—*The Rig Veda*
Translated by Ralph T.H. Griffith

Karma for Truth

This is a very powerful form of karma. The universe only understands the truth because it responds to its vibrations and energies alone. If you want the universe to listen to you, you have to not only speak the universal language of truth, but also follow the right and truthful path in life.

To always speak the truth is a very important practice. The ancient rishis practised this. They received profound knowledge and power. The results were miraculous.

Speaking the truth can be developed through self-discipline. We all tend to lie—even for small things, such as the answers to 'why were you late?' or 'why could you not complete the work?' or even 'what were your scores in the exams?' Most of the time, it is totally unnecessary to lie. Petty lies can turn into a habit.

People also lie through exaggeration. For example, when we are asked a question like 'how many places did you visit during this trip?' Instead of speaking the truth, which is 'three', sometimes people end up saying 'five'. There is no benefit to doing so and is completely unnecessary. The other person really does not care how many places you visited, whether it is three or five. You must realize that this is also a lie. If it becomes a habit, then you will begin to lie all the time. Such a habit is dangerous. By developing such a habit, we lose our power and connection with the living universe. Even when you tell the truth, people feel as if you are lying. You then get in the habit of doing negative karmic acts without realizing it. It is always better to reply correctly than to utter a lie. Lying makes you mentally weak and less confident. You lose your own respect and self-confidence, which will reflect in your personality. In time, other people will also lose their respect for you.

Now, to understand the power of telling the truth as a habit, one only needs to recall the words of Shri Shri Paramahansa Yogananda who has said: *'If you habitually speak the truth all the time, whatever you say will come true.'*

This means that when the truth is spoken by a person who always speaks the truth, the universe listens and makes it happen.

For example, in ancient times, people used to seek advice from the rishis whenever they were faced with a problem, or needed some help. The rishis blessed them and those the rishis blessed were immediately benefited. Whatever the rishis commanded, the universe would make it happen. This is the power that comes from continually speaking the truth. The universe makes it come true.

KARMA AND YOU

We can all develop the habit of speaking the truth. We will see its benefits. Whenever you try to make something happen, you will see success. You will be respected by those you meet. Your aura will reflect your sincerity and people will be instantly drawn to you. Whenever a truthful person enters the room, the place lights up with his vibrations. If we follow the principle of karma for truth, miracles will take place.

'The best way to test your own inner strength is when you speak the truth on all occasions.'

—*Shri Shri Paramahansa Yogananda*

Healing Karma

You must have noticed that some people heal faster than others. What are they doing differently?

Those who do not heal quickly are not serious about themselves and their bodies. They do not change their negative habits, do not discipline themselves, and they have no control over their diet or their exercise. The universe listens and their ability to heal is reduced.

Since they do not heal, they get depressed and, almost in a cycle, the immune system too weakens. The body forgets about its ability to heal itself.

Such people also grow old faster.

People who heal quickly are doing the right karmic acts in order to restore themselves. They are positive; they control their diet, exercise, read up on all there is to know about their problems and follow the doctor's orders seriously. This proactive karma towards their own health surely brings good results. These people decide to get to the bottom of their problems and tighten their belts to combat the disease. They are determined to heal themselves. This is the right karmic route to take towards your good health.

People who grow up in homes where there is love and happiness have stronger immune systems. When a person is very sick, he can recover faster if he receives love from his spouse, family and friends as his will to survive increases, and his immune system kicks in and keeps him healthy.

In our daily life we must have noticed how some doctors are more successful than others when it comes to healing people. Patients say that some doctors have the healing gift and their patients are happy and content with them. There are usually long queues outside their clinics. Why is this the case?

This is because these doctors practise the right karma towards their patients. They do not prescribe unnecessary medicines. They always try to do the right thing and give the correct advice. They do not chase monetary gains, but make sure that healing is their first priority. Their vibrations work towards healing the patient. This positive karma gives them the power and energy to heal. Such doctors also do not charge fees for those who cannot afford to pay for their services. They are charitable and harbour goodwill in their hearts. This type of karma gives them the power of healing. Most patients who consult these doctors feel that they will be cured, and so it happens.

'An unlimited source of protection for a man lies in his strong thought that he cannot be affected by the disease.'

—*Shri Shri Paramahansa Yogananda*

'The consciousness or manifestation of disease is nothing more than an obstruction created by wrong human thought and negative karma.'

—*Shri Shri Paramahansa Yogananda*

'The mind has greater power than medicines.'

—*Shri Shri Paramahansa Yogananda*

Karma and Thought

The Sanskrit saying goes, '*Yad bhaavantad bhavati*', which means, 'as you think, so shall it be'. If you generate positive feelings, then positivity is what you will receive.

Since our thoughts ultimately determine our lives, karma begins with our thoughts and desires.

Karma does not mean physical acts alone. It also includes what you think and your intentions. Thoughts have vibrations, just like actions. Good and positive thoughts will also attract good and positive results.

KARMA AND YOU

Thoughts are a very strong force and full of potential. Your thoughts are ultimately responsible for everything that happens. Thoughts create reality. Your good thoughts are good karma and your bad thoughts are negative karma.

Sometimes, you do good karmic acts but with the worst of intentions. This karma may not yield any good results. You must do, think and feel from the core of your heart when you undertake any action. As the Buddha has said, 'We are the results of our thoughts.'

Desires are also karma. If actions are propelled by desire, it is karma. Be careful in what you desire and the means you use to achieve it.

Even more subtly, karma is determined by our motivation. It's the thought behind the thought that matters.

Our thoughts are a part of the omnipotent universe and higher consciousness. You become your own enemy when you limit the power of your mind and thoughts.

KARMA AND THOUGHT

Swami Shri Yukteswar Giri used to say, *'If your will is clean (ethical) and strong, whatever you imagine will be created for you.'*

In the same frame, we should stay away from negative people because they sap your thought power. Surround yourself with positive people. Meditate to improve your thought power. When your intentions and thoughts are right, your mind can intuitively become creative and generate ideas for innovation.

Every time you worry, your mind suffers and loses some of its power. If you meditate and strengthen your mind, you can be rid of depression and negativity. Shri Shri Paramahansa Yogananda has said, *'You must never admit defeat (mentally)—once you have admitted defeat, you are defeated.'* Make your thought and willpower strong enough to achieve anything that you want in life.

'All thoughts vibrate eternally in the cosmos. Control your own destiny by changing your thought.'

—*Shri Shri Paramahansa Yogananda*

'The universe begins to look more like a great thought than like a great machine.'

—*James Jeans*

Karma and Your Personality

Often, when somebody walks into a room, everyone around can feel their appeal and their positive aura. At other times, everyone notices the heavy, negative aura around a person. You can always feel the vibrations of the personalities doing good or bad karma.

Good and positive karma will make one's personality likeable and trustworthy. The person doing good karma also attracts positive vibrations from the people around him.

Such a person will radiate good vibrations wherever he goes. People will be naturally attracted to him. This is because every thought and action does have an effect on every cell of the body. Good karma will affect the body and personality in a positive manner. The eyes and face act like a mirror of one's thoughts, which reflects in your personality.

The fruits of good karma are also evident in one's body. For example, a person may look more youthful and age gracefully, i.e., without any stress lines on the skin and face, and with fewer wrinkles. This is because they don't feel stressed and instead attract positive vibrations from everyone they meet.

Consider the novel by Oscar Wilde, *The Picture of Dorian Gray*. As the story goes, the protagonist of this book gets an age line on his face and skin every time he lies or does a negative action. This phenomenon is actually true in real life. Negative actions cause stress and guilt. This causes depression, health issues and ageing.

Hence, we see that people who perform the right karmic acts and have the right karmic thoughts are always radiating positivity. Their personality glows and they are sought after by everyone. You can always sense their warmth as soon as you meet them. They have a positive effect on everyone around him.

You should aspire to be like them.

'Wrong actions cause negative or evil mental vibrations that are reflected in your whole appearance and personality.'

—*Shri Shri Paramahansa Yogananda*

'Your thoughts and emotions, like waves, ebb and flow in the facial muscles, continuously altering your appearance.'

—*Shri Shri Paramahansa Yogananda*

Karmas That Are Confusing

Karma can be confusing. Sometimes it yields results that are difficult to make sense of. By the law of karma, sometimes the reactions that are expected to take place do not happen. This can be confusing, but there is a very sound reason for it, and can be easily explained by an example.

Sometimes, you see a man with negative karma accumulating a lot of wealth. You wonder how this is happening. He should be getting negative results instead.

The reason is that the man with the negative karma is still working hard to earn money. He is

KARMAS THAT ARE CONFUSING

not only dreaming and thinking of earning more money, but also working tirelessly to achieve this goal—sometimes even by the wrong methods. He is actually doing great karma towards earning more money, but not otherwise. His hard work (a karmic act) towards earning money yields results and he becomes rich. People who are aware of his negative karma often respond by saying that he should not be rich because of his lack of ethics.

However, we have to remember that a man does many karmic acts—some good, some bad. Each karma can be strong enough to produce results. The good results that someone with a lot of negative karma may witness is only short-term gain. In the long run, if he has been unethical, he will definitely lose his ill-gotten wealth. His negative karma will also bring him sorrow. Money thus earned can be lost in paring business losses, treating sickness and fighting court cases, among a host of other reasons. Despite earning a lot of money, he may ultimately be unhappy—some may even suffer from depression—and feel that his life is not as fulfilling as he had expected it to be.

Both types of karma have a result. It may take time but karma always catches up.

'You will get what you deserve.'

—Anonymous

Karma of Goodness

Good, genuine people who lead a balanced life without hurting anyone and by always speaking the truth will find that their power over mind and matter grows daily.

Goodness has to come from the heart, from within. The aura of such a person will be clean and bright. His aura will instinctively attract all around him. People will be drawn towards him; they will want to become friends and will feel happy in his company. Such people increase their inner energy and others can feel it too.

What are the traits of such a person?

Good people practise kindness, gratitude, forgiveness, care, honesty, philanthropy and service without bragging about it and without turning their backs on those who ask for their help.

All these karmic actions bring happiness and contentment. Whether you are wealthy or poor, if you are happy you will know that you have led a successful life.

When my father died, we discovered a black diary in his cupboard. This diary contained a list of names of many people to whom he had loaned money to start some business or a retail shop. We knew most of the people and we saw that they were all doing well in their ventures. However, my father never told us about this. My brothers and I got together to decide what we were to do with this book and the amounts he was owed.

Finally, we arrived at the conclusion that since our father himself had not informed us and kept it to himself, we had no right to ask for these loans to be paid back. He had given these loans to help people and it was his personal karma, and this did not involve the family.

Acts that are done without expecting anything in return are a true sign of good karma.

'When we choose to act to bring happiness and success to others, then the fruits of karma are happiness and success.'

—Deepak Chopra

Karma and Food

You are what you eat. Each cell of the body dies and is replaced in seven to ten years. Your renewed cells are made up of the food you eat. Your choice of food makes up your karma.

If you are a non-vegetarian, you must understand the processes that take place before the meat comes to your table. When an animal is slaughtered, the creature feels fear and rage. These emotions cause their bodies to be filled with adrenaline and other toxic chemicals. Each cell of their body is in a state of terror and anger. When we eat this meat, we are also digesting the frantic terror, anger and fear of

KARMA AND FOOD

these animals. We too imbibe these feelings and it reflects in our relationships with our family and friends and can ruin them. Digesting animal protein every day can actually harm the body and make you age faster.

You can see this in the way animals behave as well. Herbivorous animals like cows, deer and sheep are very calm and docile. They have no fear. They do not run away when approached and can be befriended. On the other hand, predators like lions, tigers, alligators and so on are carnivorous. They are always angry, aggressive and ready to attack anybody approaching them. This is what we learn from nature and the animal kingdom.

If you do make the choice to become a vegetarian, you will reap its karmic benefits. Foods like vegetables, grains, seeds, fruits and nuts give you all the nourishment and energy you need. These foods are made from the energy of the earth and the sun. This is what we need to keep our bodies healthy. Vegetables, fruits and nuts have more fibre and give you protection against cholesterol, diabetes and heart problems. Vegetarians are calmer, relaxed and less stressed because they don't eat animal products, thereby avoiding the toxic chemicals found in dead animals.

There is yet another choice to make for better karma. You can choose to fast once in a while. Fasting cleanses and repairs the body. Toxins are burnt and organs have time to repair themselves during the fast. It also helps reset the immune system of the body, increase willpower, burn fat and improve cognitive abilities. Fasting once a month can do wonders for your health.

Making good choices when it comes to food can add up to good karma towards your body and good health.

KARMA AND FOOD

'Tell me what you eat and
I will tell you what you are.'

—Antheline Brillate Savarin

Karma and Arrogance

Arrogance is a negative emotion and leads to bad karma. It stems from the ego, which in turn fuels a sense of self-importance and superiority. This sense of superiority inflates the ego and makes a person act out of pride.

An arrogant person considers himself to be a gift from God. He is self-obsessed. He craves admiration and hero-worship, and is generally angry and rude with others around him when he does not receive it. Arrogant people don't give credit to other people. Even if they are initially successful, in the long run they do not receive respect and love from others.

KARMA AND ARROGANCE

They lose themselves and their soul. Such persons are not liked, even within their communities.

Arrogance does not go unnoticed. The universe recognizes it and takes note of this negative karma. The cosmos treats all humans equally and tends to balance arrogant behaviour.

Acts of arrogance convey negative vibrations in interactions. These negative vibrations start to affect an arrogant person's destiny; they make him depressed and ineffective. This ultimately brings him down to the ground. But he still may not realize why this has happened to him. He does not realize that the negative vibrations he has received can do so much harm. The accumulated negative vibrations can make a person ill, unhappy and even bankrupt. They can make him feel unwanted and alone.

Arrogance can take many forms. The most common form of arrogance is associated with wealth and power. People who are wealthy and/or powerful constantly desire praise from others. They start speaking down to people, being rude and taking centrestage. They are always talking about their achievements and rarely recognize their mistakes. This triggers negative energies. Nobody likes them, even though sycophants feed their egos. In time, arrogant karma can destroy such a person's wealth and reputation. It is very important to stay humble when you are successful and enjoy the goodwill of people around you. This will help you grow further in stature. Look at some billionaires around you: they are extremely humble and donate a lot of their wealth for good causes, thereby accumulating positive karma for themselves.

Arrogance is seen in other aspects of life too. Some people are arrogant about their beauty and others are arrogant about their intelligence. Arrogance can be seen in people who are stronger than others, better off, or those who are in positions of power.

One of the worst forms of karma is spiritual arrogance. Spiritual gurus are supposed to be pious, humble and caring of all; they should teach others and uplift people. Instead, sometimes, so-called gurus act 'god-like'; they put themselves on a pedestal and expect everyone to worship them. For them, it is not about spirituality but business. They treat the rich differently from others. This is not the sign of a true spiritual leader.

Finally, remember that arrogance does not go unpunished by the cosmos. All negative energies received by the one who is arrogant lead to his downfall. Arrogant people lose their strengths and soon become unhappy and frustrated.

If we want to be happy in life, we must stop every once in a while and check our karma and ask: Am I being arrogant?

'Pride is the greatest barrier to wisdom.'

—Shri Shri Paramahansa Yogananda

Karma and Gossip

Many people gossip as a habit. Some do it for entertainment, some do it to hurt others or out of jealousy. For some, it is just second nature.

When people gossip, they are actually saying 'I am better than you', or 'I am superior to you'.

This simply goes on to feed one's ego.

The worst kinds of gossip are rumours. A rumour generally harms the person's reputation and has a bad emotional and mental effect on the receiver. It is but a pastime for those who have nothing to do. People who spread rumours have a negative mindset. The gossiper is actually twisting the truth to harm people.

At other times, people indulge in gossip for fun or entertainment. It may be fun for those gossiping, but it is agony for the one being discussed. They can be driven to depression.

Most of the time, when gossip travels from one person to another, some extra 'untruths' are added to it along the way. In the end, the truth has been twisted so much that it becomes totally ridiculous. Each person who passes on the gossip lies a little to make it more interesting. Sometimes, it may also provide sadistic pleasure to put people down. Such people are doing negative karmic acts.

They glorify themselves, boost their own egos and lie outright. All this negativity adds to their karmic account.

We all should remember that every human being is a part of the divine. By gossiping about him, you are actually gossiping about the divine himself. This is bad karma.

A day will come when rumours will float

about the gossiping soul as a consequence of his own actions. He may be made to feel like a fool. People will laugh at him. He will then have to face what he has been doing all along to others. This is the karmic consequence. Karma is watching and hearing all that we do and say.

KARMA AND GOSSIP

'Any time you talk badly about someone, you actually shorten your life force and endanger your ability to draw trusting friends and the ability to be well spoken in future times. And no one will believe what you say.'

—Jetsunma Ahkon Lhamo

'To be aware of a single shortcoming within one self is more useful, than to be aware of a thousand in somebody else.'

—His Holiness the Dalai Lama

Karma: Free Will and Destiny

Our destiny is the sum total of all our past karma in this life and the ones before that. Our destiny is decided by our karma. We all have the power to change our destiny by doing the right karma. Thus, we can change our future if we want to.

Our destiny is not left to chance; we create it with our actions and thoughts.

To ensure this, the divine has given us free will. We can use our free will to choose the right

KARMA: FREE WILL AND DESTINY

path in every decision, activity or relationship. Ultimately, we have to use our own judgement for every decision we take. This decision, whether positive or negative, is our karma, which will then create our destiny.

You can use your free will to do good karma; you can even neutralize your bad karma and correct your destiny. Many people place their destiny in the hands of fate and astrology, not realizing that it is actually in their own hands—it is their free will. Some say that it was down to luck, but they don't realize that these situations too were self-created. The divine has made us all equal. He does not make one rich and another poor. His laws are always just. He allows us to create our own destiny by giving us free will.

Of all the living things on earth (such as plants, animals and humans), only we have the gift of free will. It is because we have been born with the intellect to decide between right and wrong. Our future is guided by the path we choose to walk on.

This path leads us to our destination and destiny.

Here I would like to share an example from my life.

Our company's first general manager was a very pious and religious man. He was extremely dedicated to the company. Hard work was his karmic act.

He had two sons. Since he was like family to us, the company decided to employ one of his sons at our Kolkata office.

One day, when my father returned to Kolkata, he realized that the general manager's son was missing from the office. As he enquired into the matter, the general manager told him that he had fired his son. My father was astounded!

'Why did you fire him?' he asked.

The general manager said that his son had not been working well. If people noticed and commented upon it, saying that the son had been employed due to his father's work, it would dent his own reputation and his ability to get work done from others.

KARMA: FREE WILL AND DESTINY

You rarely come across such people!

Many years later, the situation changed. We decided to transfer two of our companies' showrooms to the general manager's two sons. The two of them worked hard and became millionaires. Our general manager was very happy and satisfied with the result of his decision. Good karma ultimately wins!

Today's decision and action taken with our free will is our own doing. You can make any choice you deem fit. But yesterday's action and their karmic reactions are not in our hands. It has already become your destiny.

We can always study our past actions and their results and see what has gone right or wrong. Thus, we can use our own free will to change our present actions. This will promise us a better future. We are continuously writing our future with every action, thought or desire.

The best time to teach our children about the concept of free will and destiny is when they are young. Destiny is the good and bad effects of karma. They will then learn to navigate their own lives and write their own destinies. We must not misuse our free will. This is the only way to shape our future and our destiny.

Today's action (karma) will determine your tomorrow. Yesterday's karma is your destiny.

'The law of karma is inexorable and impossible of evasion. There is thus hardly any need for God to interfere. He laid down the law and, as it were, retired.'

—Mahatma Gandhi

Divine Karma

What karmic acts can we do to realize divine presence and grace? What can we do to put an end to all our past karmic debts?

Only when there is self-realization of the divine, and we know that we are a part of this omnipresence, can we be free from our karmic debts.

The Bhagavad Gita, one of India's ancient and revered books, talks about three ways to attain salvation.

The first is the way of 'bhakti'. This refers to complete love and devotion towards the divine.

KARMA AND YOU

When a man thinks, acts, dreams and breathes only through divine love and nothing else, he is then in communion with the divine. He then knows that not only is he a part of the divine, he himself is divine.

The second way of divine realization is 'gyan', which means knowledge. When a person attains universal knowledge, wisdom and truth by working towards it—through meditation or by any other means—he becomes a self-realized person. He now understands the divine, he understands himself, he understands all the truth of the cosmos. Then he can be free.

The third path is of karma. This refers to the righteous thoughts and actions of an individual. Even in an unfavourable position, a karmic person is always doing the correct and right karma. This action is the fundamental truth. He will then have no karmic debts and will become a realized person.

One can ask: if karma/action is supreme, then why are there three ways for self-realization?

DIVINE KARMA

Which is the best way?

Actually, all three ways follow the path of right karma. First is the karma of love and devotion, second is the karma of attaining knowledge, and the third is the karma of right action. In all the above three ways, the individual is doing the right action/karma to find the divine.

Every kind of thought or action is connected to the divine.

'If you know that everybody is an expression of God, then to be angry (with) or unkind (to) anyone is to be angry or unkind with God.'

—*Shri Shri Paramahansa Yogananda*

Towards Karmic Balance

Karma can guide our lives. For this to be possible we must begin by understanding the consequences of our actions.

Having read this book, you should be able to recognize the consequences—whether good or bad—and make the right choices to find ultimate happiness and success. If you can understand this, your future is secured.

We all believe in physical laws such as gravity. Gravity is why we don't jump off rooftops, expecting to fly. Likewise, you too should follow the universal laws of karma to avoid unpleasant situations.

TOWARDS KARMIC BALANCE

Although we cannot change the consequences of our past actions, we can always choose our present actions and their future results. If you find yourself down on your luck and caught in a pattern, it is a sign that you should introspect and get down to working on that particular problem/karmic situation.

Our job is to respond to karma with the right attitude, only then will divine grace free us from all karmas.

We keep inquiring:

What is the purpose of my life?
How can I change my destiny?
How can I be at peace with myself and the universe?

We can do so by simply balancing our karma, just as I have explained in this book.

Remember: we all start as pure souls. Karma starts moulding us according to our actions. It influences us, whether positively or negatively. This forms who we are in the present and determines our future. Take charge of your own karma!

'That dynamic will is what makes one man rich, and another man strong and another man a saint.'

—*Shri Shri Paramahansa Yogananda*

Bibliography

Man's Eternal Quest, Paramahansa Yogananda, 1 October 1982, Self-Realization Fellowship Publishers (first published 1975)

Divine Romance: Collected Talks and Essays on Realizing God in Daily Life (Collected Talks and Essays), Paramahansa Yogananda, 1 November 1996, Self-Realization Fellowship Publishers (first published 1 March 1987)

The Story of My Experiments with Truth, translated by Mahadev Desai with Shriman Narayan as General Editor, Navajivan Publishing House, Ahmedabad

The Path to Tranquility: Daily Wisdom, Dalai Lama, 27 August 2002, Penguin Books

The Physiology of Taste, Jean Anthelme Brillat-Savarin, 4 October 2011, Vintage

'The Spiritual Law of Success', programme aired on WXXI-TV, 16 March 2019

The Mysterious Universe, James Jeans, 1937, Penguin Books

The Rig Veda, translated by Ralph T.H. Griffith, Evinity Publishing Inc, 1.0 edition, 11 March 2009

See You at the Top, Zig Ziglar, 25th Anniversary Edition, 26 June 2000, Pelican (first published 1974)

The Holy Bible, 1 October 2017, Fingerprint Publishing

1